REVIEWS
OF
DREAM

I've never been big into poetry, but Frank Bolaji Irawo has beautifully
shifted my experience with it!

Helen Amery

I love your work, Frank; it's always so moving and thought provoking.
And am loving the book cover! What I always find so wonderful are the
preamble, the comment made in passing or the crack in the sidewalk
that sparked such deep observations. I cannot wait to order a copy!

Kendra Parker

A lovely compilation of fascinating and insightful poems that give the
reader the opportunity to explore, express and challenge their views on
the world...and begin to live
a transformational life.

Chantel Hall-Reid

I love the way how the poems give you a kick start in thinking about own patterns and behaviours and the questions and exercises add onto that by guiding the reader how to explore that thinking in detail. I started reflecting of how many things I need /want to change for myself but also who else in my surrounding could benefit from reading the book as they might be at one of the decision points in the book. Further, I love how the book guides you but never judges any behaviour and instead gives advise on how to overcome and better one's life.

Stephanie Shah

WOW! The gentle clear flow of this book can really transform any readers life. Not to forget the poetry that compliments each exercise, allowing the reader to experience a quiet, disarmed, peaceful state that only enhances the profound positive and constructive outcome of answering these relevant and important questions.

Shelly Allmark

DREAM

Manifest Your Path
To
Joy, Peace and Contentment

By
FRANK BOLAJI IRAWO

DREAM
Manifest Your Path To Joy, Peace and Contentment

Authored by Frank Bolaji Irawo

©copyright Frank Bolaji Irawo 2021

Cover art work & design Marcia M Publishing House, back cover art work:Emma Chaves

Edited by Marcia M Publishing House Editorial Team Published by Marcia M Spence of Marcia M Publishing House, Oldbury, West Midlands the UNITED KINGDOM B69

ISBN 978-1-913905-66-8:

MARCIA M
PUBLISHING HOUSE

www.marciampublishing.com

DREAM

Manifest Your Path
To
Joy, Peace and Contentment

By
Frank Bolaji Irawo

Poems to Transform Your Life

Part Of the **CALM SELF** Series

CONTENTS

DEDICATION

Dedicated to my grandmother, Grace Olufumilayo Sotade, a truly special soul. Her life taught me that you do not need a lot of money to transform your world, just genuine love, care, and concern for humanity, something we all have in abundance if we look within. She left a legacy that lives on more than thirty years after her death, as she received from those with resources and used it to benefit the less fortunate. Those are lives that will never be the same again because she cared enough to make a difference to them.

ACKNOWLEDGEMENT

Thanks to all the wonderful people who have added to my life and supported me along the way to writing this book. I am grateful to my wife Yvonne and children Joshua and Melina for their unyielding support, believing in me and putting up with me being holed away for all those hours working on this project.

My mother, Ibiyemi, for carrying on the legacy from my grandmother showing me and my siblings the value of living a life that serves others and leaves them better than when we meet them, and for her constant encouragement and calling me to a greater vision of what is possible.

My sister Tayo and brother Ayodeji for their companionship in the journey. To Paul Anderson Walsh for calling out my writing gift, pointing out that I should start blogging (I was so clueless, I had to look up the word in Google), that got me hooked on writing.

To my very first boss, Steve Elliott, for showing me what it is to be a true professional. That was great advice to read my emails back before sending. Who knew? Still using that one today!

My fellow Barefooters for being the testing ground for my poetry and encouraging me with their wonderful feedback. To Barefoot

Coaching (led by Kim Morgan) for putting on events by the likes of Pete Mosley and Jackee Holder that nurtured the seed, honed the skills, and fostered the belief that I could do this!

To Camila Goytacaz who spoke this book into existence; Angela Gordon who challenged me to commit to a date and Claudia Smith for being my earliest cheerleader for this project and her input into the format of this book.

To my Sainsburys Tech family (Stuart Richards, Tesh Dave, David Hobday, Richard Cortes and many others) for creating a space where I could bring my whole self to work and share my writing gift.

Thanks to Marcia M Publishing for bringing this book to life and Tunji Olujimi for the ingenious idea that led to the creation of the D.R.E.A.M framework. Emma (Loizides) Chaves for the use of her wonderful artwork.

Thanks to my IGC church family for all their support and encouragement and to everyone else whom space constrains me from mentioning but, nonetheless, contributed. I am so grateful.

PROLOGUE

After over twenty years of personal development and serving people in several spiritual communities, I decided to pursue my dream of becoming a life coach. In my bid to secure enough residual income to replace what came in from my then role as Project Manager in Tech, I made many questionable financial decisions that brought me to the precipice of bankruptcy. My dream looked much further away than when I started working towards it.

Coming to terms with where I found myself financially was very difficult and I was at a very low point emotionally and mentally. To help me process, I decided to journal what was happening, how I was feeling about it and any insights that came out of my self-reflection.

It proved to be very therapeutic as it helped me think out loud, make sense of how I was experiencing life. Writing things down helped me see clearly what was occupying my thoughts and to explore my inner motives and bias. In the process, I became aware of beliefs and inner drivers present in my subconsciousness that might have otherwise been hidden.

Words have the power to awaken insight, invoke imagery and experiences from your past and can open a new door of awareness that could initiate inner transformation.

As I began to come out of the haze, I saw the crisis as a gift to expose the inadequacy of my then beliefs and lead me back to the light of my true self. I realised that I had been building my life on a foundation that was neither robust nor sustainable. In my quest to "make it" I was not paying attention to much else. I was sleepwalking through life.

Without those experiences, I would not be the coach I am today. What I went through gave me empathy for others, led me to learn a lot about how we experience life and forms the basis of my work today. In hindsight I realised everything had been "perfect". I had not failed the first time: the real training of life had just begun and led me to where I could serve others powerfully.

It is my privilege to share these poems and exercises with you in the hope that it serves you in your journey from disappointment to live out your dreams, while sparking your creativity to put more light into the universe in the service of others.

Like a chain reaction, we can all experience transformation and, while so doing, transform the lives of millions across the planet. All the proceeds from the sale of this book will go towards supporting worthy causes across the globe (see Appendix A for more details).

GETTING THE MOST FROM THIS BOOK

You can read this book as a collection of poems you can keep coming back to when you need inspiration to continue moving in the direction of your dreams regardless of the disappointments experienced along the way.

For your convenience, space is provided for reflections, insights, and new thinking, or you can choose to use a separate journal.

We are all creatures of creativity and I hope that this book inspires your own poetry, sketches, mind maps or whatever else takes your fancy. Creativity has been found to reduce anxiety, depression, and help people cope with stress and process trauma.

You can dip in and out of the poems as you see fit using the poem index at the back of the book to find what you need.

I have grouped the poems together into sections that make up the **D.R.E.A.M.** framework which, together with the accompanying exercises, make this a self-coaching tool designed to take you from where you are to experiencing your dream life, if you follow through on the reflections and take action.

Discovery - Know where you are now

Recovery - Get the gold from the past and move on

Envisioning - See what is possible

Action - Do what you know to do now

Manifestation – Experience your dream life unfolding

The poems in this book can also be used like a collection of coaching cards.

Below is the D.R.E.A.M. Framework for using these poems in a coaching session. I use these same poems in my coaching practice, and they have been very effective in helping my clients see new concepts, shift perspective, and gain insights that create transformational results in their lives.

Discover what area/topic the client needs/wants to explore

Read the relevant poem that covers that area/topic using the poem index

Explore what resonates or creates resistance for the client

Assess what insights have arisen for the client

Make a next steps commitment plan with the client

There is a poem index to the back of this book for your convenience.

DISCOVERY
Know where you are now

> ## When the student is ready
> ## the teacher will appear.
> ## When the student is truly ready...
> ## The teacher will Disappear.
> ## – Lao Tzu

Whatever stage of life this book finds you, it is the right one for you. This book is in your hand because you are ready to start living the life that you only ever previously dreamed of. Let us start by becoming aware of where you are and how you got here.

In your earlier years you were most likely filled with optimism and dreams of a wonderful life and then "life" itself got in the way and the harsh realities of needing to make a living started to dawn on you. You started to neglect the things you got so much enjoyment from.

It often takes a crisis or significant event to wake you up to the reality of how far you have drifted from your aspirations. You may have been seeking validation from "success" as defined by external markers such as fame and fortune.

Questions are a great way to get to the wisdom in us and inspire creativity as they task the brain to search for answers.

You are about to create a space to ask questions that will tease out answers for reflection and develop a view as to what your next steps could be to start living in a new reality.

Section Content

SLEEPWALKING

Sleepwalking, just kept walking
As time after time, I keep slumping
Life's day-to-day needs navigating
Sudden thud and I'm sleepwalking no more
Pieces of me in crisis sprawled across the floor

Awake to what passed me by
The dreams left behind
In places long forgotten
Gasping for air in space confined
Seeking release with Keys stuck
Under piles of hats not long been juggled

Sands draining, not much remaining
What say you start living
Awake from sleepwalking
To live the life, eyes wide open
No longer unconscious but breathing

Smelling the roses, basking in the light
Savouring the moments
Where magic happens
Living, alive, feeling and thriving
Memories made, no longer retracting
Inspiring others to awaken from sleepwalking

Crisis has a way of slowing you down to see what all along has been there, but you have been ignoring or taking for granted.

Become intentional about noticing the small details in your life. Make a list of one thing each you can be grateful for in your:
1. Relationships
2. Health
3. Career/Work
4. Contemplative/Spiritual life

SOMEONE
I USED TO KNOW

There may just be some pulse left
Features barely recognisable
Emaciated from years of neglect
Stuck in the corner with no attention
Atrophied from years of no stimulation

What a crime to humanity
One once so full of life
Until life itself got in the way
Deflated and left in quiet desperation
Drained of energy for yet another recuperation

Dying embers of a once bright spark
Barely visible from years of deprivation
The world denied the verve and creativity
The fun, joy and laughter
That was such a revelation

In the interest of humanity
Some food, some air and exercise of the brain
Maybe just then
It may just breathe again
Live again
Skip again
Laugh again
Fill the room again
Some semblance to the one I used to know

It is easy to lose the essence of who are with all the roles you assume through life. You start living just to get through the day unscathed.

Bring back some fun into your life. Below are some things you could try. Be spontaneous. Write down how you felt after each experience.:
1. Dance like no one is watching.
2. Sing out loud like no one is listening.
3. Go out dressed in outrageous colours.
4. Try eating or doing something you have never tried before.

WHY ME?

Why me, why now?
I hear you ask
Why not you, why not now?
My own refrain
Your question so framed
A victim you remain
Answers to light a party for pity
Offering little for a forward gaze

You call it a problem
I say opportunity
Heavily impregnated with many possibilities
Which you deliver very much depends
Neurons faithful servants to where they are sent
To bring back answers to justify your pain
Or build a better future from what remains
Have your party if you must
To move forward you will need to park that bus

To embrace the chance of a new day
Send those neurons to your creative brain
Ask helpful questions such as to follow
What can I learn?
What can I do differently?
How can this serve me?
What opportunities does this present?
Hopefully by now you get the idea...
Play and get with it, have a filled day
You may be amazed by what comes your way

When things happen that you rather did not, there is a tendency to start looking for what or who to blame. This approach will predispose you to being the victim of your situation.

1. Consider a "problem" situation in your life and write down your answers to the following questions. Once you have finished with all the questions, then reflect on any common themes, lessons, or takeaways:

    A. What can I learn?

    B. What can I do differently in the future?

    C. What opportunities does this present?

2. Compose a poem, write a short essay, a story or draw a mind map or visual to capture what came up for you.

HOW DID YOU GET HERE?

How did you get here?
Which path did you travel?
How long did it take?
Who did you meet?
Who have you parted with?
What have you learnt?
What grew?
What died?
What transformed in you as a result?
What are you grateful for?
Where next?

Questions are like servants that reach out into your brain to find answers. The quality of the questions you ask determines the depth of the answers your brain returns.

This exercise will help draw out the transformational effect of your experiences.

1. Write down your answers to each of the questions asked in the poem. Once you have finished with all the questions, then reflect on any common themes, lessons, or takeaways.

2. Compose a poem, write a short essay, a story or draw a mind map or visual to capture what came up for you.

THE STORM

Got the plans from the designer
It set out elaborate recommendations
About how to build a house to last
There were references to a strong foundation
Before the walls go up
Seems like it'll cost a bomb and take so long
Quite a bit of bother
All for a part of the house
Nobody will ever see

That all said and done
The fact remains; the house is mine
I can build it exactly how I want
My aim is to impress, the Joneses next door
With a house, that will make heads turn
My priority is set, for what to spend
It's outside, inside and then beneath
The sooner the better, for the walls to go up
Take as little time, on the parts that can't be seen

It wasn't easy
But we got there in the end
My stunning house was now complete
I lost count of those, who stopped to comment
On just how beautiful a house, it looked
So it should be, as no cost was spared
For it was to reflect, the glory of my wealth and taste
It had been standing some time, no sign of it falling
I knew the designer had just been overcautious
There really was nothing, to be worried about
All was well, like the calm before the storm
That's when all hell let loose

An almighty storm, like never seen before
Seemed to rise out of nowhere
I felt reasonably confident
Apart from the faint echoes of my designer's advice
Well, the rest is history
I took shelter in the Joneses' house

We've cleared the rubble
Remnants of an expensive lesson
I'm ready to build again
To never ignore the designer's advice
Insure against the storms of life
Drive those foundations deep
No cost or time spared
So I can provide the shelter
For other unwise neighbours
When the storms, hit again

Is your sense of security built on things outside of your control?

1. Write a list of unfortunate events that have taken you by surprise and the outcomes that transpired.

2. Review the generated list from the step 1 and ask yourself the following question. "What would I need to change to build better resilience in each of these areas?"

3. Put a plan in place to start implementing the list from step 2.

ENOUGH

When so and so happens, then I will ...
Fill in the blanks as you know what I mean
Be fulfilled
Be happy
Be complete ...
The list goes on with the end so tantalisingly out of reach
Pushing into the distance what dwells deep within
Imbued with the seeds of your own greatness
Hard to find everywhere else what only you can grant
Permission to declare that you are enough

We were born enough and then we have been conditioned by our social systems to seek validation from our achievements. We then adopt rules regarding what we need to achieve before we allow ourselves to experience contentment.

1. See how many more you can add to the list below of all the things you are waiting to happen before you allow yourself to feel enough.
A. Get a good job.
B. Get married.
C. Have children.
D. Gain financial freedom.

2. Rewrite the list from step 1 as follows "I am enough now even if I never {insert item from your list here}"

NOW OR NEVER

Looking over there yonder
Where the grass is always greener
In the hope all will be better
Than all that is here now

Oh how familiar that story seems
Told of this moment back then
Only to replace it with another
Waiting for the day that never comes

We seek it because we are it
Distracted from the truth of it
Seeking where Red Herrings live
Wild Goose running off into the distance

Right here, right now
Is all there ever was
As far as the breath we breathe
No longer winded from the futile chase
Awake to that which I already am

How much longer will we wait for utopia to arrive before we permit ourselves the right to experience the sense of contentment that is here right now?

1.   Make a list of three things that you enjoy doing.

2. Plan that into your schedule. Set a date to do each one at least once in the next two weeks.

RECOVERY
Get the gold from the past and move on

Life is divided into three terms – that which was, which is, and which will be.
Let us learn from the past to profit by the present, and from the present, to live better in the future.
– William Wordsworth

After taking the time to reflect and discover what has transpired, it is time to Recover the gold from the past and move on to what supports your future.

No matter how dark things get, there is always a future to look forward to. After night comes day. If you follow the pathway pointed out by this book, you will come out energised and heading for the life you dream of.

The things that have happened in the past are useful for reflection and learning to avoid perpetuating unhelpful patterns, but then there comes a time when you are faced with the decision to move on. To let go of past hurts and leave the past where it belongs.

You do not have to journey alone. Find those that can support you in this journey who can provide perspective and context with hope and wisdom.

You are now ready to start seeing and embracing what is possible for your future.

SECTION CONTENT

DARKEST HOUR

In my darkest hour so bleak it seems
Appearing as if there is no way out
Then nature comes to my rescue
Remembering the sun is never gone
No matter how dark night gets
Over the clouds it arises to light the dawn
Revealing the pathway for the new day
So panic fades as innate wisdom shines through

It can often be hard to see beyond present negative situations. Things are not often as bad as they seem or feel. Deep within your inner essence you are still okay, and the moment will pass.

1. Reflect on the last time you felt how you do now and write down responses to the following.
A. What caused you to feel that way?
B. What happened to turn it around?
C. What positives came from it?

2. Sit and watch the sun rise and reflect on where the sun has been. Compose a poem, write a short essay, a story or draw a mind map or visual to capture what came up for you.

THE GOOD, THE BAD AND THE UGLY

Good things come out of situations that look ugly
We see the ugly and call it bad
But if we look more carefully
We can see right through the ugliness
To the good that it obscures

As long as the universe has our back
Everything we face has a lesson to teach
Even if it wears an ugly mask
That does not make it bad
We no longer see the bad in the ugly
But the good that lies therein

If you look deeper than the surface appearance, you can unearth what gifts are presented in your situation.

1. Reflect on an unpleasant situation you faced recently and write down answers to the following:
A. What have your learnt about yourself?
B. What have you learnt about others?
C. Who can you support with what you have learnt?
D. Who does it help you develop empathy for?

LESSONS FOR LIFE

The school of life is in session
Lessons to suite all budgets
You decide the price
Your expense or that of others

Take it Free from good advice
Learn from the mistakes of others
You could of course choose to pay
With your very own mistakes
You never fail, you just retake
Be warned, every retake costs more
How much are you willing to pay?

You may be engaging in patterns of behaviour that increase the risk of producing a negative effect on your experience of life. Lovingly accepting the part you played, if any, in creating that experience will empower you to make better choices in the future.

1. Reflect on any repeating unpleasant outcomes you are experiencing and write down answers to the following:
A. How are you contributing to the outcome?
B. What occurs to you to do differently?
C. Whose example can you learn from?

POINT OF PAIN

Pain points
Don't miss the point
And focus on pain
Get the point
Get to the point
Address it
That's the point of pain

Physical and/or emotional pain is never desirable but has a purpose to draw your attention to something that needs your focus or may just be indicating how much weight you are putting on something.

1. Explore areas you experience pain in your life and write the list below:

2. Take each of your answers from step 1 and reflect on the following:

A. What is this pain trying to tell me?

B. How am I responding to this pain?

    I. Denying it

    II. Numbing it

    III. Addressing it

3. Reflect on your responses to steps 1 and 2. Write down any changes you are inspired to implement in any of these areas.

GIANTS

Standing on the shoulders of Giants
Never-before-seen perspectives coming into view
Insights once obscured now exposed
Seeing further than ever before

Standing on the shoulders of Giants
Felt more capable than I ever could
That which I feared lost its power over me
Seeing it for the impostor that it was

Standing on the shoulders of Giants
Grateful that they would let me
As I perused endless possibilities
Filled with hope of a better tomorrow

Standing on the shoulders of Giants
I got help and persevered
Gained courage and found my feet
To stand taller than ever

Standing on the shoulders of Giants
Was the next upcoming generation
That shoulder was mine
For all humanity to stand taller
So none has to start from scratch

You never have to face life alone; find someone you can confide in to support you in the journey. There is power in sharing your experience.

1. Write a list people you can trust and share your aspirations and obstacles with them(see the epilogue at the back of the book if you want to engage the support of a coach).

2. Make a list of people who have helped you in the past and write a note of gratitude to acknowledge their contribution.

UNFORGIVABLE?

Can't believe you would even suggest it ...
To forgive and validate the evil done to me
To forgive and betray the memory of my loss
To forgive and deny the gravity of my hurt
To forgive and release them from this guilty sentence
To forgive and not have the story to tell of the wrong done to me

It may very well seem unforgivable to you
The question on the table is can you really afford not ...
To forgive and invalidate the hold it has on you
To forgive and realise it's not them the poison in you is harming
To forgive and be unshackled from the sentence of sour memories
To forgive and let your healing begin
To forgive and take responsibility for starting your journey into the light
A gift only you can give yourself

Not forgiving past hurts hold you captive to the past and affects your ability to move on with living your dream life.

1. List below the painful/hurtful things that have happened in the past that are you still dwelling on.

| |
| |
| |
| |
| |
| |
| |
| |
| |
| |
| |
| |

2. Write a declaration of forgiveness for each of the things from step 1:
"As a gift to myself I this day {date} choose to forgive {offender} for {thing that caused offence} as I let go of every offence and embrace myself with compassion."

THE DEAD

The unhelpful past is gone
No longer here
What do you do
With the dead?
Dead by design
No use for living
Bury the dead
Lest it causes a stink
Making life unbearable
For the living
Let the dead be buried
To make way for the living

Having extracted value from the events of the past, it is best to move on and stop rehearsing it. The present moment is our gift to enjoy.

1. Make a list of the painful/hurtful things that have happened in the past that are you still dwelling on.

2. Write each of the items from step 1 out as a declaration as follows: "I choose to leave {the details of the event} in the past."

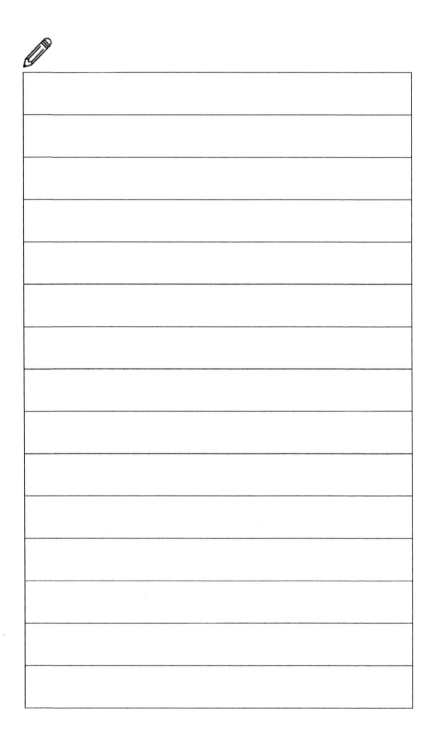

ENVISIONING
See what is possible

> **Don't underestimate the power of your vision to change the world. Whether that world is your office, your community, an industry, or a global movement, you need to have a core belief that what you contribute can fundamentally change the paradigm or way of thinking about problems.**
> **– Leroy Hood**

What contribution do you want to make in the world? There is a good chance that everything that you have experienced to date is preparing you to do just that!

It is time to explore what are your dreams and how your gifts and experiences have helped prepare you to start living them. Developing a vision of where you are going acts as a beacon or north star drawing you towards your destiny.

There can be a sense of apprehension when you commit to doing what is required to live out your aspirations, but do not let that stop you. Stretch and take the next step and start a ripple that has the potential to spread out and transform your part of the world.

Are ready to show up and act so that what appears to be a dream starts materialising as a reality?

SECTION CONTENT

DREAMS

Dreams, the birthplace of all reality
Not every dream becomes reality
But there is no reality
That did not first start as a dream
Dream on and create the opportunity
For endless possibilities
To create new realities

1. Suppose tonight, while you are asleep, the miracle happens and everything you ever wanted is there. Your dreams have come true. When you wake in the morning, how will you be able to tell that the miracle has happened?

After the miracle, ask yourself and write down your responses to:
• What will I see that is different?
• What will I hear that is different?
• What will I be that is different?
• What will I feel inside that is different from the way I feel now?

2. Now ask yourself and write down your responses to: What would the other people in my life see, hear, notice, that was different? Think about each of the people in your life and see yourself after the miracle from their point of view, imagining what is going into their eyes and ears, what is going through their mind as they deal with the new you. Think about what they would think about your behaviour, attitude, values in your new life. Think about how you would behave, knowing what they think and see, and what you would have to do to make them see you behaving that way.

SUCH A TIME AS THIS

"Who knows? Maybe you were made ... for just such a time as this."
(Esther 4:14, MSG)

Seemed innocuous at the time
All those jobs I did
The many skills I honed
The people along the way
How I was guided through
This maze called life
To arrive here
For such a time as this

So it all unfolds
Piece by piece
They come together
O' what a gift this Hindsight
As I begin to realise
Nothing was ever wasted
All I have been through
Accounts for such a time as this

I am living it
It's happening to me
Walking in my destiny
Who would have thought it
The Universe working through Me
To achieve more than
I could ever dream
At such a time as this

I'm so blessed our paths have crossed
Laid out as a Master Planner
Hatched this wonderful plot
To sharpen one iron with another
That creation might be enriched
To release a sweet aroma of love
At such a time as this

Everything you have experienced and everyone you have crossed paths with has played a part in who you are today.

1. Reflect on all the things you have been through and how it has prepared you for this season of your life.

2. Reflect on all the people you have met and how they have contributed to preparing you for this season of your life.

SPECIAL

"Oh yes, you shaped me first inside, then out; you formed me in my mother's womb. I thank you, High God—you're breath-taking! Body and soul, I am marvellously made! I worship in adoration—what a creation! You know me inside and out, you know every bone in my body; You know exactly how I was made, bit by bit, how I was sculpted from nothing into something."
(Psalm 139:13-15 MSG)

A gift to the world
A unique expression
Peculiar to the core
None like you in all the earth
From your tip to your toes
No recycled mould in sight
You are truly extraordinary
There is no other in the many billions
Who can rightfully claim to be you

Your call if you accept
To display the splendour
Of a masterful creation
There is only one you
All others can only imitate
You the only original
Here to Reflect
This manifold glory
The way only you can

Eternity waited for you
To reveal to the world
The unique creation that is you
Completing yet another part

Of this exquisite tapestry
Bringing us your variant
Of exquisite fragrance
That we may celebrate you
The only you there will ever be

Hear the hollow sound
Resonating from the emptiness
Trying so hard to be accepted
In the land of clones
Try as much as you may
It never seems to be enough
To impress the unimpressed
The bar just keeps rising

Hear this plea, heed this call
Return to us, the one you stole
That we may celebrate
The greater One in you
In Him you are always accepted
No hoops to jump through
Loved unconditionally
With such unrelenting intensity
Return to us, the real you
The one and only you
Just as you are

If you show up embracing your uniqueness, you will draw those that resonate with your style.

1. What is unique about you and makes you stand out, that you can serve others with?

2. Which group of people are already attracted to you and see you as a resource?

3. How will they learn enough about you to buy/hire from you?

4. What are next steps you will stake to start your venture to serve others?

GIFTS

You need to know how precious the gifts you are carrying are
They are destined for the yet unknown and the yet unborn
They are a deposit of the creative flare
To bring to fruition works of beauty and poise
Creations that leave their mark on the consciousness of humanity

Start believing that what you carry is powerful
What you carry is effective
Give it voice
Give it form
Those ideas plead to be set free
That they may mingle in the hearts of mankind
That it may influence the way they see
That it may influence the way they speak
That it may affect their deeds
To change the world we live in, one person at a time
Each life worth every bit as much as ours

Inspiration is the breath of creation
To begin the process of birthing invisible ideas into reality
We the chosen wombs to nurture the seed to fruition
Capture those ideas
Give them voice
Give them form
Let us all behold the beauty of it all
You are a chosen one, believe, conceive, and deliver!

You are endowed with many gifts; they are vehicles for bringing your dreams to life.

1. Do a gift inventory.

2. How are you using each of the gifts listed in step 1?

3. Where do you experience resistance when opportunities arise to put those gifts to use?

4. What stories are you telling yourself about why you are not putting those gifts to use?

5. If you were to let go of those stories from step 4, what would become possible for you?

PRISON

Caught in a Prison of my own making
Erected with bars of my own design
No obvious way out
The original intent to protect me
Now conspires to constrain me
Hostage to that which was meant to preserve me

Living under the sentence of its blackmail
Afraid to reveal its ploy to the world
Thriving only possible through freedom
From this persistent tyranny
Re-framing this scene to a new reality
Where fear no longer terrorises me

Firing up brain cells to mobilise positive energy
Signalling the chance to grow instead
Getting curious about what triggers me
Fact checking elaborate tales of impending travesty
Mitigating true concerns
To feel the fear and press through
To serve the world from a place of liberty

Fear usually comes from your brain trying to protect you from perceived danger. Consider the relevant risks and take necessary precautions, but do not let it stop you.

1. What are you most afraid of when you contemplate stepping out to fulfil your destiny?

2. What disempowering stories are you telling yourself that keep you stuck, and are you willing to let go of them?

3. Write down one small action you have decided to take in each area where you have been stopped by fear in the past.

FISHBOWL

Set in my ways, unwilling to change
Always done it this way
Found my comfort zone
Why rock the boat
Gotten used to the same scenery
Round and round I go
Swimming in my own fishbowl

Scary thought, what might happen
If I were to leave my bowl
Lost in the great and vast ocean
Having to deal with the unknown
Requires trust in the unseen
Letting go of my current "security"
Swimming in my own fishbowl

There must be more to life than this
There is a deep part of me, that calls out for more
An inner witness that I was made
To do more than exist
What have I to gain or lose?
I'll never find out
Swimming in my own fishbowl

Sink or swim, here I go
Abandon my fate in the hands of the universe
I and the ocean from the same source
Time to start on this adventure
Discovering what life awaits
When I'm no longer
Swimming in my own fishbowl

There is no substitute for stepping out of your comfort zone. Make the jump; the universe has your back.

1. What are the things keeping you from jumping?

2. What is your head saying about what may happen if you make the jump?

3. What is your heart/gut saying about making the jump?

4. Which small steps are you going to take to follow your heart/gut?

THE RIPPLE

"We are in one of the greatest fields of service, helping others live a fuller life." – Frank Bolaji Irawo

Making the world a better place
One person at a time
Once the pebble drops
The ripple starts
No control over how far it goes
That's the way influence grows
Completely out of control
Start one now!

One small action you take today could be the catalyst for change in your life and that of others. The influence generated develops a life of its own and how far it goes nobody knows.

1. List the kind of changes you would like to see in the world.

2. Who are those you can serve today to start a ripple?

ACTION
Do what you know to do now

> **"Do the best you can until you know better.**
> **Then when you know better, do better."**
> **— Maya Angelou**

The insights you have gained from the journey so far have set you up for making changes that lead to the transformation that will materialise into the life of your dreams.

It starts with a decision but will need to be followed up by corresponding actions that originate with you. It may not look like much is changing to start with but stick with it as you lay new foundations for your dream life.

A lot of energy is wasted trying to be what you think you ought to be based on made-up stories and assumptions. This divests your energy and dulls the potency of your actions. Show up as you are.

Lean into the discomfort of doing new things that start showing up on your pathway. Things are rarely as bad as the mind paints it and the only way to verify that is to just do it.

Viewed in retrospect, you will discover how far you have come. Do not forget to enjoy the journey so that the whole of life becomes an adventure of a lifetime.

SECTION CONTENT

POWER

What know you of it?
It dispels the darkness
Brighten eyes to see the unseen
Casting off its cloak forever
Poking holes in long held assumptions
The apple cart well and truly tipped
Spotted sacred cows sprawled in its wake

Breaking free from doors wide open
Making way for a future
Never before imagined
New tracks laid to lands
Once forsaken

Hidden in plain sight
Right up close to your tips
In sharing it expands
Transforming the planet
The power of knowing
Right here, right now

New insight creates momentum for change which can happen in an instant or over time.

1. Write down any new insight or perspective that has come to mind.

2. Make time to reflect on each of them and ask the question, what could be different because of this?

CHANGE

My world changed
Yet everything remained the same
That which is now seen
Could no longer be unseen
The elephant in the room
No longer invisible
The blur came into focus
As the scene became clear
New eye piece, new view
Assumed certainties no longer safe

The villain of the piece
Was no longer without
The chance to journey towards better
Paid for by my current discomfort
Great opportunity
To own what is mine
The power of change
Now firmly in my gift
To show up differently
With fresh energy
To start the chain of change
So nothing remains the same

Embracing change is a choice and the first step to experiencing it.

1. Which areas of your life can you take responsibility for and start making small changes?

2. Write down one small change you can make for each area from step 1 and start it today!

ACORN

Once upon a time
A great big oak from an acorn did grow
The seed impregnated with great potential
Physical eyes could not yet see

It, having been sown
To give it the chance to grow
Joins the Magic of the universe
Sinking roots deep down
While passers-by went about their business
Unsuspecting of the greatness
Hidden in plain sight

As time passes, seasons come and go
Till heads turned reflecting in awe
How this great tree was hidden
In an acorn so small
What is growing in you?

It can take time to see the outcome from each action you take to create change. Do not give up.

1. Where in your life can you see small shoots of improvement?

2. Do something special to celebrate those small shoots/wins.

BEING ME

"... And you shall know the truth, and the truth shall make you free" (John 8:32 NKJV)

"Have they gone?"
"Can I take it off now?"
It weighs a tonne, this mask that I wear
It's the only way I know, to hide what I see
Just so I don't have to face me

I had visions of perfection, doing all things right
I shouldn't let the side down
Mustn't give a bad impression of the team
Everyone else seems to be doing better than me
At least, so it seems
It is hard to tell who is wearing one like me

I could not afford to be me, a price too high to pay
All those tongues wagging, and the disapproving looks
From those who had this whole thing, down to a 'T'
It was clear to all concerned, that I hadn't done enough
Trying much harder to perform
Earning the right to show up as me

Disappointment lingers on inside
I'm not who they want me to be
So I sport this false accessory
At least I fit in, as long as I'm not alone with me

My actions showed me who I was
A memory of who I used to be
The more I look, the more I see
Till I know who I really am

A wonderful creation full of love
Then and only then can my actions fall in line
With the reality at large within me

A human being, not a human doing
Hence, I know, I am, so I do
O what Liberty I have
From the truth that has set me free
It's OK just to be Me!!

Being free to show up as you are, releases more energy to manifest your dream.

1. Write a list of the personas you have created to hide your true self.

2. Reflect on the personas identified from step 1 and write down what triggers each one to show up.

3. What stories are you believing that are making you afraid of showing up as you really are?

4. Write down one small step you can take in each area of your life where you have been hiding to start showing your true self.

LEAN IN

Leaning into my discomfort
Exploring unfamiliar terrain
To dare to step beyond uncertainty
Out into the wild unknown
Expanding my horizon
One step at a time
Everyone as uncomfortable as the one before
Defying the Naysaying voice
Predicting my doom

How fleeting and selective memories can be
It was only the other day it played the same tune
Trying to dissuade me from what was then new
For what was then foreign I now call home
Drawing from my deep well of courage
Cheerleaders in tow
The universe at my back in case I fall
Regardless of outcome I will know more
I dare to call its bluff and start to lean in

Beyond that gnawing discomfort
Lies my point of growth
To experience more
To learn more
To manifest more
To reach more
To serve more
To love more
The space of endless possibilities
All waiting for me
As I keep leaning in

To grow we need to learn to embrace discomfort, as it often indicates the opportunity for growth.

1. Where are you feeling the discomfort?

2. What could become possible for you if you leaned in?

THE DEED

I feared the shadow
Of the ominous deed

Stalking my thoughts
For days on end

Evading the light
Of what could be

In elusiveness
Its powers grew

Finally for a dare
It I did Confront

By its spell
I was no longer bound

Having no where
Else to hide

Powered by the courage
From the Deed now done

There is no substitute for doing something. It is the only way to get better.

1. Reflect on times when you felt scared to act. Make a list.

2. For each of the answers from the previous step. Reflect on the learnings from the instances where the outcome was not as bad as you thought.

MYTH

"Perfectionism, Procrastination and Protection all begin with the same
letter" – Dr Susan Rose

Must be perfect
Inch perfect in fact
Not a thing out of place
Just exactly as I imagined it
No point in starting
If I cannot get it bang on!

Still waiting
No telling
How long before Perfect comes along
Almost there
Just a few things missing
From how I imagined it

Answer me this
If you will
If perfect is so perfect
How come it's not the same for all?
Who needs this mark?
That can never be hit?
Rather convenient, don't you think?

A perfect nothing is still nothing and will not deliver any value to you or anyone else for that matter.

1. List the things you are avoiding completing, by trying to be 'perfect'.

2. If you did what you can with the best knowledge and skill you have right now for each of the answers from the previous step, write down the value each would deliver.

3. Close your eyes and visualise those you serve experiencing the benefits right now and write down what it felt like.

4. Convert each item from answers to step 1 into a declaration as follows. I am going to {insert action here} now because it will {insert those you serve and the value they will get from it}

MANIFESTATION
Experience your dream life unfolding

"It's only after you've found what you want inside of you that you can find it outside of you."
— Cory Groshek

So far it appears our dream life is something we make happen and it relies on external events for it to materialise. From this paradigm it can often feel like it is a lot of hard work to get "there".

When you visualise your dream life, you taste a bit of the experience you are looking to enjoy. That experience has always been there for you to have, but your stories and beliefs about what needs to happen on the outside first form a barrier to living it now.

If you are willing to consider that the universe is calling you into the experience of a rich and fulfilling life where you embrace all that it brings your way, you get to participate in the unfolding of the universe in the service of all and embrace the privilege of it.

Enjoy the experience of life that it is laid out in front of you and celebrate the small miracles all around you. Relax into doing what comes to you in the moment without attachment to the outcome. This will lead to you experiencing your most productive state.

You are already enough as you are. Do whatever you choose to do because you know that you are enough, not to convince you or anyone else of it. Allow inspiration and love to drive you. Your dream life is unfolding before you with everything you do. Every action is making a difference in the world.

SECTION CONTENT

I WANT

I want it ...
I need it ...
It ... is due to me
I deserve it ...
Yes indeed
I want it ...
And I want it ... now

Who is the I?
Bound in time
Separate from them
Lost in the haze

What does it want?
That is not already here?
Looking in the wrong place
For what is not lost

To know of it ...
Is to know it ... is
For how else
Could it ... be known?

There is value in enquiring into the relationship between external events and the experience you have of them.

1. What are the things you believe you need to have to live your dream life?

2. Close your eyes and visualise that those things have already happened and write down how they make you feel.

3. Reflect on whether those experiences come from the things outside of you or from within.

PURSUIT OF HAPPINESS

In the pursuit of happiness
Lies the belief unexpressed
Denying the innate essence
From which the knowing springs
That eternal well of abundance
That is happiness itself
Pursuit, the barrier embraced
To obstruct its natural flow
Cause it just doesn't feel so
In the moment of confusion

Your belief about happiness and where it can be found will influence your experience of it.

1. What are a few things that have made you unhappy?

2. Reflect on instances where the things listed in step 1, have not resulted in unhappiness.

3.   What are a few things that have made you happy.

4. Reflect on instances where the things from step 3, have not resulted in happiness.

5. Reflect on whether the happiness come from things outside of you or from within?

THE PERFECT UNIVERSE

The universe so benevolent,
Perfect as can be
May not serve up what you want
But you'll get just what you need

That pretty much is the point
To expose the delusion
That it panders to how
You think it should be

Billions of years in the making
Pregnant with the treasure of endless wisdom
You presume to give it
A piece of your own mind

It is here to present you
The opportunity
To Discover the real, you
The essence of your innate brilliance

To break the falsehood of a fixed self
Ever resisting and constricting
To embrace the totality of all possibilities
Experiencing the full spectrum of your being

Consider that your dream life is whatever the Universe is wanting to unfold through you and all you need to do is trust and flow.

1.   Reflect on the events of your life that you resisted in the past.

2. In what way have those events added value to the experience of life you have now?

3. How can you start embracing the things you are currently resisting?

LAND OF TRAVEL

You've travelled near
You've travelled far
You've travelled here
You've travelled there
You've pretty much travelled everywhere
You still haven't found what you are looking for
The utopia at the end of that Galactic rainbow

In anticipation of the great climax
Reserved for the place called "there"
Perchance you may have missed
The land of travel itself
Each interaction a journey
Each new culture a revelation
Exploring differences as sameness
Experiencing the joy of serendipity
As the universe surprises you
In ways only it can do
Every day created anew to experience
When next asked where you need to get to
You can answer, "I don't very much care"
I'm in the greatest destination of all

We miss so much of the everyday fun of life because we live it in transit mode. Missing the precious little moments in search of a big climax that may never come.

1. Set an alarm for every 15 minutes and note down what you were thinking of. At the end of the day identify which of those thoughts were about the past, present, or future.

2. Reflecting on the results of the previous exercise, what proportion of your time is spent in the present moment?

3. Set an alarm for every 15 minutes. Write down what is new and unique to the moment and celebrate it with gratitude.

4. Become aware of and note down events that appear as coincidences (serendipity in action) and celebrate them.

NO TRYING

Out in the yard I was
At rest in place, I saw it
A tree with flowers in bloom
Nothing else it could do
It is what the season determined
In it, I saw no trying

On to its branches there flew
A bird adorned in white and blue
Its flight as graceful as can be
Perched at rest with no sign of stress
For it was what it knew to do
From it, I saw no trying

And so, for a treat it stretched
Picking from the abundant bloom
To meet its need for the moment
After it had its fill, it flew
For there will be a next meal
In that moment, there will be no trying

As natures knows to be
What the universe sets in motion
For design decides what being reflects
To embrace the wise unfolding
So, there is no place for trying
Just the glorious emergence of being

There is a wisdom to the unfolding order of the perfect universe. If you trust this by following your gut, intuition, etc, you can manifest your dream life without stress.

1. Reflect on past experiences of trusting the guidance of the universe by following gut/intuition and the outcomes you experienced.

2.   What areas of life are you experiencing as hard work?

3. For each of those areas identified from step 2, what is your gut/intuition leading you to do instead?

FLOW IS ...

Flow is bliss
As time ceases to exist
In the moment when
Awareness is transfixed
On what the soul seeks

Flow is a state of mind in which a person becomes fully immersed in an activity. Mind and body are in tune and tasks feel effortless It is an optimal state for delivering peak performance with ease.

1. Reflect on times when you have been in flows and note what typifies the conditions under which you experience flow.

2. Observe times when you struggle to enter flow and observe is any of the below are present (can you come up with other flow inhibitors?):

A. Overthinking

B. Attachment to outcomes

C. Fatigue

3. Based on your observations from steps 1 and 2, make a list of things you can do to increase you chance of entering the flow state.

MYTHICAL BEAST

Searching for that mythical beast
Without it I'm told I can't be complete
With all others I must compete
To find that which has been missing of me

Untold harm incurred in its pursuit
Banks emptied; souls vanquished
Once dear relationships laid to waste
No rest for the soul that yearns to be filled

Countless people line well-worn paths
Some crawl, some walk, while others fly
United in the seemingly never-ending quest
Bent on finding and taming this elusive beast

Come what may, no matter the cost
The promise of utopia fuels the drive
This many people just can't be wrong
All hell bent in service of filling the void

Each step I take seems to bring me close
Till right before my eyes, it seems to mutate
Perchance the description given crafted to mislead
I dared not quit, failure the antithesis of what I seek

Some days I arise feeling like this could be the one
Catch up with the beast that fits the bill
But the promised euphoria fails to persist
Like the great Houdini it eludes my grip

Surrendered to my fate it never to find
Taming that mythical beast was never mine
Returning home in despair only to find
The beast was always here, and I was it

Clue – The beast hides in plain sight behind the first letter of each verse.

Find pleasure in the everyday beauty around you, do not get caught in the rat race, trying to outdo others or conform to their definition of success.

1. In what areas of your life do you tend to compare yourself with others?

2. What endeavours are you currently engaged in that are driven by you trying to prove something to someone else or gain their approval?

3. If you never achieved anything else in life, what would you celebrate about who you are now?

EPILOGUE

SECTION CONTENT

WORLD CHANGERS

I changed the world
In truth I had no choice
As egg and sperm contrived
To seal my fate
How can it remain the same?

I changed the world
In truth does it really matter?
For whatever course I take
Be it for better or worse
How can it remain the same?

I changed the world
In truth I did try not to
My energy I could not contain
Reaching, touching, transforming
How can it remain the same?

I changed the world
In truth I can choose
Showing up fully
Embracing all there is
How can it remain the same?

I changed the world
In truth we all do
We the veil of flesh no longer bearing
Now at large in stories being told
How it was forever changing

Whatever legacy you want to leave behind, start in proportion to what you have now! That way, there will be no regrets.

1. If you were given the choice to leave this world right now, what would be the most important things that you would regret not having done?

2. From your responses to step 1, what can you do now to start making a difference?

3. List the existing networks you have and put a message out to each with your intentions to see who can support you in making it happen.

THE DANCE

Welcome, step in
This space belongs to you
To unpack the stories
The ones that shaped you
To venture down paths less trodden
To explore landscapes from heights
Rarely reached
The bird's eye view of what there is
To start that journey
To where you want to get to

Let's make this space safe
As confidential as can be
One that works for you
With unconditional positive regard
No judgement from me
So you never have to worry
About showing the true you

A quiet Hush fills the room
Where would you like to begin?
The floor is yours
I ask, you speak
As you speak, I listen
As the answers pour out of you
I hear you; I see you
I support
I challenge
Space and time feel endless
As we go even deeper
Right to the roots
Trusting instincts

Being ever-present
Reflecting back what I see
All unravelling in real time
Our only plan to respond to what shows
up The pathway opens for us to take
Venturing to see where it leads

Listening intently
Responding truly
Engaging fully
Embracing the not knowing
In hindsight we arrive
To destinations beyond your desires
Cause we dared to trust
Responding to what's birth of the moment
In the magic of the dance

WORKING WITH A COACH

Completing all the reflective exercises and taking the corresponding actions should see you closer to your dream life.

Working with a coach, however, offers you the opportunity make progress sooner on your journey, as they are trained to help uncover blocks, gain deep insight, and facilitate transformation.

When looking for a coach:

1. Check that they are accredited by a professional coaching association such as the following:

Association for Coaching (AC)
UK International Coach Federation (ICF)
Association for Professional Executive Coaching and Supervision (APECS)

2. Find out about their results and previous client feedback.

3. Spend time in a discovery session with them to check that they are a good fit for you.

AUTHOR'S BIO

FRANK BOLAJI IRAWO

Transformational Coach, Speaker, Writer and Poet.
I am a certified coach with the International
Coaching Federation. My coaching style is
empathetic, incisive, and transformational and is
aimed at engaging the whole self. I am passionate
about supporting Leaders experiencing stress and
burnout, who have gotten lost

in the demands of work and life to reset, gain clarity, live with greater ease,
reconnect to their true inner self, and rediscover their passion for life
while increasing their impact and enjoy this experience called life. This is
achieved through Powerful Transformative Conversations, Reflections,
Tools, Exercises, and action plans that help them to discover their
underlying views about how they are experiencing life and then embark
on a journey of sustainable transformative change through mastery of
new perspectives and practices.

With the right support, you can discover how to experience life in a way
that connects you to your true essence and enjoy real happiness, real
security and real balance from within.

Transition from	To	By creating	From
• Mental suffering from being	• Conversations to	• Space to	• Exploring the Mind,
• Against what is	• Ascend	• Embrace	• Awareness,
• Never at ease under the	• Living	• Life	• Surrender and
• Illusion of	• Miserably	• Fully	• Experiencing flow
• Control			

I help my clients explore:

♀ How life really works.

♀ How to become aware of what is really going on.

♀ The true essence of who you are.

♀ How to create the space to focus on what matters most.

♀ How to transform your experience of life and of those around you regardless of circumstances.

Once you see these, life becomes easier, light-hearted, connected and fulfilling.

Here is what some of my clients have to say:

"... My work life and personal life are so much richer now as a result" – **Digital Product Owner at Sainsbury's**

"..working with Frank there is a deep wisdom that comes from the wealth of life experience he has had, that creates a real depth to each coaching session. From the coaching sessions I have had with Frank, I walk away having really got to the heart of my limiting beliefs that are at the core of my soul and having tangible and practical solutions as well as a positive mindset to tackle the challenge I brought, head on." - **Group Vice President People and Culture EMEA at Discovery Communications**

"In my experience, Frank is an incredibly intuitive & insightful coach. His style is very natural & calm and he creates an environment where space and time feels endless. His really made me think and helped me access thoughts and feelings that resulted in me finding greater clarity and creating a tangible action plan. This was both enlightening and empowering and has enabled me to open new doors & create opportunities for myself in the area we were exploring..."- **Head of Learning at Danone**

"I would absolutely recommend Frank to anyone who is looking for some clarity, to develop a deeper understanding of their approach to professional and personal challenges, their triggers, attitudes and thought processes that are not serving them, connecting more effectively with responses to feelings, situations, and relationships. I can't thank Frank enough for the positive changes he has helped me to realise" - **Director at MAYHEW LONDON LTD**

If you would like to find out more about my work, you can reach me as follows

1. Email me at contact@letmebefrank.coach

2. Connect with me on LinkedIn at **www.linkedin.com/in/frankbolajiirawo** or

3. Join our Life Transformation Experience Group on LinkedIn to continue this exploration for the latest updates about events and future book releases

Book a free discovery call at
https://calendly.com/letmebefrank/discoverycall
or

Index of Poems

Additional Resources

I hope you have enjoyed this book and are that much closer to living your dream life. This is the first in the CALM SELF series of reflective books that cover different aspects of life. Planned future titles will cover themes such as:

Leadership
Relationship
Creativity

Resources that complement this book:
Life Reboot Guide – Request this free guide on how to create the space to experience your best life at
https://www.thecalmself.com/the-life-reboot-guide
or

Books
The Untethered Soul - Michael A. Singer
The Surrender Experiment - Michael A. Singer
The Inside Out Revolution - Michael Neill
The Space Within – Michael Neill
No Self No Problem - Chris Niebauer
The Greatest Secret – Rhonda Byrne
Working out Loud – John Stepper
The Gifts of Imperfection – Brene Brown
Give and Take – Adam Grant

Appendix A
The CALM Self
Foundation

Inspired by my grandmother – who left a rich legacy touching so many lives with her kindness, care, and concern despite not having much money – I have realised that whatever legacy I wanted to leave, I had to start in proportion to what I have now! This means that I can die any day not having any regrets.

Therefore, I have formed The CALM SELF Foundation to create transformation in the lives of people across the planet by supporting charities aligned to the United Nations Sustainable Goals. All proceeds from this book will fund this work.

Visit **https://www.un.org/sustainabledevelopment/** to find out more

or

It is my dream that, together, we will raise many millions of pounds to transform the lives of so many people right across the planet while creating the opportunity for everyone who reads this book to experience transformation that will create positive change in their world.

Together we can send this book viral by letting all our networks on all platforms know about it and giving it as a gift to those we think may benefit from it.

The following are the charities that will be funded by 100 per cent of the proceeds from the sale of this book. They support causes that align with The United Nations Sustainable Development Goals and all the donations will go towards their causes and not their operating costs.

1.   Charity Water

Aligned to THE UNITED NATIONS SUSTAINABLE DEVELOPMENT GOAL # 6 - Clean Water and Sanitation

Visit **https://www.charitywater.org/frank-bolaji-irawo** to find out more

or

2.   Lend With Care

Aligned to THE UNITED NATIONS SUSTAINABLE DEVELOPMENT GOAL #8 - Decent Work and Economic Growth

Visit **https://lendwithcare.org/** to find out more

Or

3. The Blue Fund

Aligned to THE UNITED NATIONS SUSTAINABLE DEVELOPMENT
GOAL #4 - Quality Education
Visit **https://www.christs-hospital.org.uk/support-us/blue-fund/**
to find out more

Or

4. Green pastures

Aligned to THE UNITED NATIONS SUSTAINABLE DEVELOPMENT
GOAL #3 - Good Health and Well-being (Housing)
Visit **https://www.greenpastures.net/invest** to find out more

Or

5.   B1G1

Aligned   to   All   THE   UNITED   NATIONS   SUSTAINABLE
DEVELOPMENT GOALS
Visit **https://www.b1g1.com/** to find out more

or

Book back cover Artwork by Emma Chaves
To see more of her work, visit **emmasfineart.com/**
or

www.marciampublishing.com

Printed in Great Britain
by Amazon